The CEO Next Door

How to beat sexism & self doubt to become a CEO

Dr. Daniela Palaez
Daniel Strandt
EJ Ellis, MBA

Our struggle isn't fair, but together we can continue to make it better.

The goal of this book is to provide inspiration and practical steps that you can take to make your climb to the top just a little easier. The world is full of advice and sentiment spoken with good intention but be weary when insight is not supported. Each critical point of guidance in this book is supported with data from resources that we deemed trustworthy.

This book is honest and open, some topics and concepts may be painful or difficult to accept, others may be infuriating or frustrating. The feelings that arise are critical to the internal assessment that is explored throughout the book. To help guide those feelings and your focus, every section begins with a thought provoking or inspirational quote to set the tone for the section.

I hope this book is as impactful to you and your life as it was for me researching and writing it.

Contents

Chapter 1: Introduction to the C-Suite 1

Chapter 2: Shaking Off Sexism 26

Chapter 3: Promote Yourself 35

Chapter 4: Be Yourself 48

Chapter 5: Package yourself as a leader 75

Chapter 6: Fulfillment of dreams 102

Chapter 1: Introduction to the C-Suite

"Because I am a woman, I must make unusual efforts to succeed. If I fail, no one will say, "She doesn't have what it takes." They will say, "Women don't have what it takes." - Clare Boothe Luc

Over the last several decades, women have been making great strides to elevate themselves from a second-place seat in business. Many women working today have carved out a great position for themselves. But while the availability of top positions for women has improved significantly, statistically there is still a gap when it comes to the higher leadership roles in business. There has been a remarkable increase in the number of women in managerial positions over the past few decades and specifically in the last few years. In 2019,

The CEO Next Door

29% of senior management positions are held by women, this is the highest number ever recorded. 87% of all global businesses had at least one woman in a top position. However, even though female managers have increased in number, the research shows that in 2018 in the major geographic areas studied, women only held 16.8% of the total CEO positions (Catalyst, 2019).

Most new management positions being created are being filled by women. The United States recorded an increase of about 4.5 million management positions from 1980 to 2010; this is a percentage increase of approximately 90%. Of those new positions, 2.6 million have been occupied by women while men occupied 1.9 million. Men still occupy 60% of all managerial seats, which is a significant decrease from the 75% they held in 1980 (Scarborough 2018).

The statistics are improving, but women still face many challenges; challenges that their male counterparts in the same field do not understand and oftentimes never experience. The issues that women face, coupled with self-doubt are the reasons many women don't attain their dreams of climbing the corporate ladder to the C-Suite. The C-Suite gets its name from the typical titles of executive managers, such as Chief Executive Officer (CEO), Chief Financial Officer (CFO), and Chief Operating Officer (COO).

Today's world is ruled by power, money, and success; to the delight of many, an incredible number of women are at the top. Women are building and conquering, however, many women still suffer from competing priorities and occasionally, the idea that it is a man's world, and they do not stand a chance of landing a high position at the top of the corporate sector. In some instances, those roles aren't obtained because of very real external forces, but on other occasions it may be because we don't realize that we are responsible for the creation of the barriers that exist within ourselves. The first step is for you to believe that you can climb and reach for anything you want. You can do it all, competing priorities do not have to be an issue and this is not a man's world, it's a world of opportunity for anyone that will take it. Believing that you do not have a place in the corporate world stifles aspirations and becomes a self-fulfilling prophecy and a barrier, it is time to eliminate that self-doubt.

It is a fact that the struggle women face to move upwards is real and continuous, but it's worth fighting for. In fact, according to a report by the Center for American Progress, there was an increase of 94% in women who occupy seats on the board of directors in the S&P 1500 companies between 1997 and 2009. Even more importantly, the number of women in top executive management positions increased by 86% in the same time period (Judith Warner, Nora Ellmann,

Diana Boesch 2018). You can be one of the women that continue to move the needle forward.

Once the decision has been made internally, the next step is to understand and obtain the skills needed to enter the C-Suite; this book will provide extensive actionable steps you can use to reach that objective. There will be many things that will change for you on your climb, but progress requires change and these changes are pivotal for the accomplishment of your goals. Remember that no one is perfect, as you climb the corporate ladder, it is about the habits you develop and the lessons you learn during the climb.

The next section will take a look at what makes it so difficult for women to elevate themselves into the higher ranks of the business world and outline solutions that can remedy these challenges. We'll begin developing an understanding of these challenges; it is important that we begin with internal challenges before trying to face external changes.

Self-belief
"Love yourself first and everything else falls into line. You really have to love yourself to get anything done in this world." - Lucille Ball

Do you lack the belief that you can become "the boss" and succeed at it? That internal belief is the most pressing issue. You may have adopted attitudes of, 'Why should I invest time attempting something I know I will never achieve?' Even when the opportunity presents itself you may shy away from it; and who can blame you - most women were not brought up believing they could take on leadership roles. Most women were raised and conditioned to become assistants rather than leaders and they focused their studies and goals accordingly. When looking at the historical career choices that many women made, this becomes glaringly evident, but it doesn't have to remain this way. Unfortunately, the perception has continued as many women see becoming a CEO as an unobtainable ambition and a challenge that they may not be able to manage.

It is true that climbing the corporate ladder is challenging, but you can handle it just as well as anyone. Overcoming this hurdle boils down to one simple solution, you must build yourself up and develop a sense of belief in yourself that is as strong or stronger than your belief in anything else. Self-realization and self-actualization help - you may have to remind yourself of your worth as you face challenges. As a woman, you must evaluate and learn to value yourself separately from how society evaluates you. From now on, continuously remind yourself of what makes you great and that when you set your mind to it, you can accomplish anything. Develop your self-esteem by fanning the fires of success with the fuel of self-belief.

This can be challenging for many women, don't worry, we will discuss self-belief throughout this book and provide steps that will make this process easier for you.

Often, when women are asked whether they feel comfortable being in charge, or if they feel more comfortable supporting someone else's goals, the typical answer isn't one or the other, it's that they have never thought about it. Only a small percentage of women ever consider the option of being a leader or have even stopped to ask themselves if what they are doing is what they want to be doing with their lives. The answer to this simple question is stronger than you might think, it can provide a pathway for women to break out of the norm. There is a need for more women to ask themselves these kinds of questions, as it will lead to the beginning of an awakening. It is almost certain that the answer will lead to self-actualization and eventually self-motivation.

Upon reflecting inwardly, many women realize they have been doing what was expected of them and not necessarily what they desired. If the answer is that you want to be in charge, then changes will need to be made. This means you will need to know what you want and apply yourself to master the skill sets needed. Now you can begin to understand that the opportunity to land the job you want exists, and it is there for the taking, but it requires crystal clear focus.

The CEO Next Door

Women are constantly made to believe that their efforts are best served in the capacity they hold, instead of chasing a dream that may not be achievable. Your efforts likely already play an important role in the company's success, but wanting to push further or becoming more shouldn't be discouraged. You can prove important in any role, even in the role of CEO, it is not a gender-related position. In fact, according to a survey by the Peterson Institute for International Economics, which covered 21,980 companies across 91 countries; having women in top-level positions increases profit margins. The study found that if a firm has at least 30% of its board members as women, it can realize an increase in net profit compared to other firms with fewer women in leadership positions (Blumberg 2018).

Many women didn't grow up aspiring to become CEO, hence their gratitude to be a part of the equation, and their willingness to stay humble and accept the position they are in. However, the opportunity exists, you can transition into a CEO role, and if the opportunity doesn't present itself, then this book will show you how to create it in subtle ways.

You'll learn how to work hard, smart and how to stand out. You'll learn that you will win more people over by being kind, humble confident and caring. You discover that nobody appreciates a hostile takeover, so be diplomatic in your approach.

With that brief exposure to internal challenges, let's look at the external barriers you will face and start to learn to combat those barriers in creative ways.

Female stereotyping
"What is sad for women of my generation is that they weren't supposed to work if they had families. What were they going to do when the children are grown - watch the raindrops coming down the windowpane?" - Jackie Kennedy

Many women were raised to believe that only men could assume certain roles, unfortunately, many men were raised to believe the same. Although these archaic mentalities have been overcome by progressive individuals, they are still fresh within the minds of many people. Society is content with the mission of a woman running the home and taking care of the children, but that is as far as they see a woman's purpose. If your goal is to run your home and raise your children, these principles apply to you as well; that goal is at least as challenging as obtaining a CEO position and is much harder to maintain. However, why can't you do both if you want to?

There are many interesting facts about women in the United States; 47% of the workforce are women, and only 40% of women are breadwinners in their respective families. On average, women earn about 79% of what men earn according to the statistics. Even when you consider college graduates, men still earn more than women by a whopping 18%. Women occupy only 21% of senior leadership positions, which is behind the global average figure of 24%. In a study which involved over 22,000 companies worldwide, 60% of them had no women representation in the board (College 2019). These are the statistics we are working to change.

When society looks at you, they do not envision you driving expensive cars, unless those cars belong to a spouse. They don't picture you owning a successful business, and they do not picture you becoming an extraordinary executive. Society rarely sees women as worthy or capable of becoming the CEOs of a successful business. This is the poison that society has developed over centuries; many women are becoming more and more uncomfortable with the expectation. This discomfort is causing a ripple effect and is bringing about a great revolution. By reading this book and acting on what you learn, you will become a part of it.

Female stereotyping will probably be one of your most difficult battles as this challenge is based on the thinking of others, which is often hard to change. Still, there are ways to overcome it. Changing a person's viewpoint in these old-fashioned thought processes might be challenging but it is not impossible. To overcome this, there are actionable steps that you can take. To influence other's perceptions in the corporate world you must portray each of these seven characteristics & actions daily:

- Demonstrate that you have more abilities and strengths than are expected of you

- Behave differently from what society commonly expects of women

- Demonstrate that you can uphold your job responsibilities

- Be punctual, orderly and thorough

- Stay focused - always keep the target in sight and work diligently toward it

- Consistently work harder and smarter than what is expected for your position

- Be involved in defining your job roles, responsibilities, and projects

If you apply each of these items, you will gain the attention needed to be taken seriously. You will begin to be viewed differently than your peers. This is a new type of thinking and it leads us to another hurdle that makes attaining this achievement even more difficult:

Equal opportunities
"Prejudice is sinful. All blood flows red. And the most harmful and foolish kind of prejudice is prejudice against yourself. Every woman is your sister, and every woman needs her sisters. So try to give other women the courtesy of your compassion, respect, and forgiveness. Love yourself despite - and because of - your flaws. Jewell Parker Rhodes" - Jewell Parker Rhodes

Everyone must pay their dues, but that is different than suffering at the hands of oppressors to reach your goal. It is crucial to understand the difference between earning your way and being abused. You should never accept unfair treatment as something that you must endure to move forward. It is not a rite of passage, you should never feel pressured into accepting mistreatment in order to achieve your goals. When you are confident in your abilities you will not accept oppression; the key is obtaining that confidence. You have more skills and talents that are applicable to the corporate world that you probably know. In fact, decades of research shows that women are better managers than men. A survey revealed that out of 27 million employers who put women ahead of their male competitors, 87% of the interviewed employers and 90% of the employees prefer women mangers due to their motivational encouragement. The employees appreciate female managers for many reasons, one being that most of them use a bottom-up management approach. Female managers also often provide their juniors with career development opportunities (Schneider 2018).

Inequality is still one of the biggest challenges faced by women in the corporate world. It puts a huge roadblock on your chances of moving forward. As discussed in the last section, historically women have not been viewed or treated as equals to their male counterpart's and have not been given equal opportunities. Some may even say that women are treated even more negatively when they work hard to prove that they are equal to their male counterparts. This may feel like you're making progress only to be beaten down for doing well. To combat these challenges, keep these suggestions in mind during your journey to CEO:

- Take a leap and reach for whatever you want in your career. Make your goals known and perform the tasks needed to reach those goals.

- Never give up. No matter what occurs, share your stories, successes, failures, and challenges, and learn from the stories that are shared with you.

- Strive to increase your level of persistence, this can work magic for you. The ongoing faith that you can obtain your desires is the path to success.

- Garner and master the skills you need to win this race. Not just practical skills, but you also need to hone the specific behaviors discussed throughout this book.

Focus on these behavioral areas:

Communication skills – the abilities to be concise, thorough, empathetic, and stern are not developed easily. Learn ways to communicate with people from various backgrounds, this will give you an edge in understanding and expressing the needs of your company, your team, and yourself. Learning to read people can be of great value and will make your interactions easier with your colleagues.

Leadership development – leaders are not born, they are created. They develop ways to teach and foster the people under them to become the best version of themselves, they are self-motivated and team conscious. A good leader will exhibit the ability to manage groups of people and projects with finesse, maturity, and creativity.

Emotional intelligence – women are often thought of as emotionally driven and at times this perception can be a major setback. Many people are disillusioned to believe that women operate off their emotions solely and therefore cannot perform logical job duties. Be assertive while still showing a sense of emotional control, this will prove your ability to handle stressful situations; this is a skill any employee in the C-suite must possess.

Focus on learning creative, productive and positive ways to stand out. In order to grow, sometimes you need to put yourself in uncomfortable situations; don't sit by idly at a meeting when there are vital topics to discuss. Speak up and share your ideas. In order to become an asset, you must be heard.

Gaining the support of other women
"Do not bring people in your life who weigh you down. And trust your instincts ... good relationships feel good. They feel right. They don't hurt. They're not painful. That's not just with somebody you want to marry, but it's with the friends that you choose. It's with the people you surround yourselves with." - Michelle Obama

It is much easier for women to advance to positions in the C-suite when they have encouragement and support from mentors and other women in the workplace. According to Bowling, 2018, mentors are critical for the professional development of women. Mentors provide a method to exercise communication skills which are essential to leadership roles. Additionally, mentors can help women acclimate to new positions faster and provided a trusted confidant that can encourage growth (Bowling, 2018).

However, that is easier said than done. One would think the fact that many women have already suffered in the workplace would make it easier for them to garner the respect and support of other women, but it often causes a very different result: competition. Building a sisterhood in the workplace can be a very difficult thing to do, but just like many difficult things, it´s not impossible. Be careful with women who work to prevent another woman's success. Occasionally you will find women that work even harder than their male counterparts to prevent your success. While garnering support from these and other women is very difficult, but like many challenges in life, it is worth the effort.

It is important to build up a network of powerful women who support other women's causes, as it will foster the groundwork for motivation as well as progressive thinking. It is true that getting over this hurdle may be difficult, but here are some useful steps to give you a head start down this path.

- First and foremost, be the example, support and empower other women. Demonstrate your support towards women, expanding their roles and lives. Be especially supportive of your peers.

- Be just. Treat others the same way you demand to be treated. This is not just towards women in the workplace, but men as well. Be fair and just to all coworkers regardless of their station, gender, beliefs, race, etcetera. That fairness and equality you exhibit is the same fairness and equality you expect to be returned. This should be exercised regularly because, first, women are trying to change inequality and bias, demonstrating these negative traits will not positively influence those around you. Work diligently to change people's perspectives by showing people that their prejudices are invalid and that you represent what you are trying to accomplish.

- Practice humility. Remember where you come from and how you got to where you are and help others to do the same. Don´t do the work for them but become the sponsor that you would have wanted for yourself back when you first began. Mentor others so that their journey might be a little more pleasant than yours was.

- Exhibit unity and togetherness, passion, excellence, and enthusiasm. This will lay the foundation for your progress. Be a part of the team and make other women feel that they are an important part of the team as well.

If there is just one lesson that you draw from this book, it is that you should heed the legitimate advice of the women who have already gone on to succeed in the roles you desire. These women will often tell you they had clear mindsets and a sharp focus on their goals, far before they ever considered becoming CEOs and taking on the responsibilities that provided them the chances they needed to prove their abilities. What this means is that the women before you were able to open up their internal dialogue and assess what it is they most wanted to achieve in life. These women will tell you that nobody else took their hands and lead them down a path toward their career choices, only that those people who offered advice became a part of their support system.

You cannot expect anyone to understand your journey, but by bridging a gap with those women who have already been through what you are about to go through, you are arming yourself with knowledge and opportunity to learn from the mistakes and successes and others.

Be Confident

"Because you are women, people will force their thinking on you, their boundaries on you. They will tell you how to dress, how to behave, who you can meet and where you can go. Don't live in the shadows of people's judgement. Make your own choices in the light of your own wisdom." - Amitabh Bachchan

The way many women are raised is a barrier to success. It can create a deep-rooted lack of confidence that affects capabilities. Fortunately, there are ways to combat this. Trying to build confidence directly is challenging; rather than trying to fight that battle, focus on striving to become comfortable knowing that there will always be people trying to distract you from your goals. Unfortunately, this often includes friends and family. The solution for this is simple, get accustomed to this fact and under no circumstances allow it to divert your attention. Go into everything you do with the knowledge that those people exist. If you are clear with your purposes and on what you are trying to accomplish, you will be successful in getting what you desire. Not everyone will like your goals or methods, but that is their problem, not yours.

Katty Kay and Claire Shipman offer some excellent insight into the value and challenges surrounding confidence. Katty Kay is an anchor on the BBC and Claire Shipman is a reporter for ABC; they explain that for years women have kept their heads down and worked hard with the expectation that eventually they would be rewarded for their efforts, yet men are still promoted faster. They found that the most critical trait that a woman in a high-level position has is confidence (Kay & Shipman, 2014).

Women are nearly universally seen as being the submissive gender and in order to break that ingrained thought process, you must not become subservient in your role, instead be confident and proactively involved. This means not just doing what you are asked but going beyond that and interjecting your thoughts at the prime moment they need to be heard. This means being tenacious; some people may misinterpret that, but you need to break out of your shell and eliminate the feeling of subservience or it will prevent you from meeting your goals.

There are three attributes that can help you to break through your insecurity in this area:

- Knowing what you are trying to accomplish and being ready to explain the reasons why you are ready.

- Being aware of strategy and technologically savvy. Your ability to show you know what you are talking about will make people see you as a knowledgeable resource, as an asset.

- Make valuable contributions to your team and company. Look for the opportunity to be valuable and seize any chance you get to showcase your skill set.

Having a strong sense of what you can accomplish and are capable of will make other people more comfortable working with and for you. But you must remember that finding your voice is not enough. You must work to have your voice heard and bring value to the table. Work to create a strong personal brand and establish guidelines and rules to follow before you begin each project.

Position yourself as an expert in your field, and always speak with confidence. Keep in mind that regardless of gender, no one wants to collaborate with someone who appears to be a weak link, even if they are not. Appearances matter; ensure that you always appear solid.

Speaking Up
"When the whole world is silent, even one voice becomes powerful." - Malala Yousafz

When presenting or speaking in front of a group of people, the fact is that many women are terrified by the possibility of becoming ostracized or rejected. However, respect is earned when someone voices their opinion and it adds value to help shape policy, workforce, and the perspective of others. It is your responsibility to make your presence known as a leader and a collaborator. Believing in your ideas is critical to achieve success when you articulate them to a group. Speak up, add to the discussion in order to show your merit on the topic and open the possibility of having your ideas utilized to create new opportunities, projects, and products. Being present in a room is not enough, bring something new and innovative to the table.

If you think you are being treated unfairly you should speak up; chances are the people who you need to impress have no idea you are even facing any form of abuse or discrimination. If you never say anything, how will they know? Do not endure more than you must just because you are trying to get somewhere in life. It is not one of the qualifications you need to have in order to reach your desired position.

If you intend on becoming a CEO, don't waiver from using your voice to better your company, especially if there are employees who are risking the company's reputation by practicing bullying. This point cannot be stressed enough and its repeated many times throughout this book; do not allow others to put you under unreasonable stress just because you desire to get somewhere in life.

Asking for money
"Women have to work much harder to make it in this world. It really pisses me off that women don't get the same opportunities as men do or money for that matter. Because let's face it, money gives men the power to run the show. It gives men the power to define our values and to define what's sexy and what's feminine and that's bullshit. At the end of the day, it's not about equal rights; It's about how we think. We have to reshape our own perception of how we view ourselves." - Beyoncé

Promotion is great and should be celebrated, but it can put a damper on things if you are not being compensated for your efforts. There are many women who face this very challenge. Many businesswomen who have moved to high level in their careers often have a barrier when it comes to compensation. This is typically either because they undersell themselves or they are hesitant to demand the amount they deserve.

Women often practice underpricing. Fortunately, getting over this issue is relatively simple:

- Be confident enough in your skills so that you can price yourself properly, which means learning about competitors and understanding the value of your talents.

- Stand firm and gain the respect of those that will support you. It is these people who will become a network and the evidence that you are creating value in your organization.

Female leaders or leaders in the making often have a fear of being rejected. It is a common internal struggle and unfortunately, rejection is something that is impossible to avoid. Learn to trust your own voice, if you do not speak up, you will never get over this fear. The fear of rejection is an obstacle standing between you and your success. It prevents you from reaching the potential you know you can achieve. This will in time prevent you from even seeing new, if you allow this to happen, all the possibilities you have now will be filtered into a small handful. Try to talk to someone about your feelings of rejection because bottling up those fears is the worst thing you can do. It will only create more self-doubt.

In the workplace, every employee has something they are afraid of, that is normal. Talk to your mentors about your fears and you might be surprised to hear them tell you about how afraid they were when they were in the same position. When you talk about your fears, it becomes less scary than it was at first. Reach out to other colleagues because they may share the same fears as you; this way you can give each other support when needed. Think of past events that have pushed your fears to the maximum level. You can successfully dismantle your fears by thinking about them on a deeper level, such as finding the point where the fear began and discovering why you've held onto it so tightly. With this technique you can start immediately, and it will begin to remove those fears one by one.

Understand and accept that when a woman struggles and seeks out help, she is more likely to seek other female colleagues rather than male ones. As a leader you should be comfortable seeking help from and coaching other women. Surround yourself with women who will not be shy about supporting and encouraging you. Strong women are not afraid to give other women assistance when it is deserved.

Reaping the rewards
"My message to women: Do what makes you feel good because there'll always be someone who thinks you should do it differently. Whether your choices are hits or misses, at least they're your own." - Michelle Obama

Unfortunately, some women hesitate to claim their own success. They do not feel comfortable taking credit for their work and do not proudly proclaim that they are fit for the job, even though they know they have what it takes to own the challenge. This may be due to the fear of being labeled boastful or conceited, however, it makes no sense to have the skills and have nobody know about them. A strategy to manage this concern is to learn how to accept credit for your work with humility and class, however, don't hesitate to be proud of your accomplishments.

- Proclaim your success, you earned it. You deserve it and you can be a beacon to other women with humility and dignity.

- Be confident you have something valuable to offer. Know that you have a reason to be where you are and rise to meet that purpose. Be content with your self-development and know that you can make a difference with your intelligence and talents.
- Gain the confidence to be noticed; people will acknowledge that you are in the room and that you deserve to be there. If you are to be the head of the organization, you will stand out and you must grow accustomed and comfortable with that. If you shrink back into timidity you may lose your chance to shine.

Chapter 2: Shaking Off Sexism

"I've always been fascinated about how much more well-behaved we have to be than men. I did get a moniker of being a 'diva,' which I never felt I deserved — which I don't deserve. I've always been a hard worker, always on time, always professional." - Jennifer Lopez

Sexism is a burning issue all over the world; as such, it comes as no surprise that it is one of the leading issues that aspiring women face today. Women can be treated unfairly because of gender and sometimes there is no way to get past it. Though equitable treatment and availability of roles have improved over time, they still need improvement. As an example of how some of those roles have changed over time, in 1980, medical and other health sectors had the highest number of women in managerial roles. In 2010, there were still many female managers in medical and general health making up to 70% of those positions. But since then, many more managerial occupations have recorded an increase in the number of women. For example, women dominate managerial roles in educational administration, real estate, human resource, and finance. However, the number of women-held CEO and public administration positions are still far less than that of men, comprising less than 25% of the total (Scarborough 2018).

This type of oppression is seen in different forms, whether it is a delay in promotion or facing criticism. Women have to develop a thick skin and learn how to shake off inevitable sexism. It is the women who learn how to shake it off and continue with their lives that prove to be strong enough to handle emotional stress.

An aspiring female CEO must learn how to master this skill because as she climbs up the corporate ladder, she will encounter this problem. Being able to combat it with tact could prove crucial to your success. For some people shaking off sexism is as simple as ignoring it and sticking to their grind, upping their game, and showing their co-workers they are strictly about business. These women just pay no attention to it and keep moving along. Some women say it is a constant struggle that they go through daily, but they are strong enough not to be hung up on it or be distracted by it. Still, there are individuals who might need to do more than that. Remember that most people are not accustomed to women taking this role and that many people may hold old-fashioned viewpoints. These people may even be your relatives or friends. When discouraged by the belief systems of those you respect it can sometimes prevent you from striving to do something other than what is expected of you.

If the people closest to you do not listen to or understand your perspective, they often will not respect your motivation. Often, a woman will have a great idea, a burning issue even, and will avoid speaking up about it. This is an internal struggle, but it is important to remember that it too can be defeated. Again, do not stay silent because speaking out is the first step to accomplishing great things.

Do not just take any advice
"Many receive advice, only the wise profit from it." - Harper Lee

When you first begin working at a company, you will likely observe that there may be room for growth. It's key to share your desire to promote with someone who can become an advocate. Listen to this person's advice but do not take every word of wisdom uttered by someone else as a solid way to earn your way to the C-suite. Be cautious about the advice you receive because sometimes the advice may be coming from people who are seeking to sabotage your chances of realizing your dreams. This person may actually feel they have your best interests at heart, they may see your dream as unrealistic and therefore harmful to you. Whatever their intentions are, it is important for you to keep focused on what you are aspiring to achieve and take all advice with consideration.

Do not be discouraged by this advice, simply pay attention and listen for the meaning and motivation within their advice. This will also give you an idea of who you should have in your circle. Take some time to step back and look at the bigger picture when considering the behaviors of others. Everyone has their own agenda and everyone is working toward achieving that. Sometimes when it appears that they are doing something because of you, they may actually be doing it for their own objectives.

Women are continually subjected to oppression because they feel that they must choose between being loved or being heard. Realize that it is our own mind that we must overcome. Everyone deserves to both be heard and loved, but it is up to you to discern the underlying motivations.

Don't be afraid to make a change
"Don't think about making women fit the world - think about making the world fit women." - Gloria Steinem

You must not be fearful of change. If you have reached a certain place in a company where you feel that moving forward is nearly impossible, do not be afraid to leave. You can voice the fact that you aspire to move up the ladder and possibly make partnerships to that end. But if you meet criticism and dead-ends, start seeking another job immediately. Everyone starts in a situation with the intent of growth, nobody wants to be stuck in the same spot forever and stunted from progressing.

There are certain qualities present in female leaders that differentiate them from their male counterparts; embracing these differences can help you create inspired change. Don´t hide these qualities; instead, emphasize and celebrate them. To fit in, many women try to adopt the leadership styles of men, thus suppressing who they actually are. Do not be afraid to be different from what is expected. You are different and you must be comfortable with that because someone somewhere is looking for something different. You will unerringly find that it is difficult to perform at your best when you adopt the behavior of others or change who you are.

There is no sense in wasting time trying to be someone you are not. You might find that you have conflicted feelings and emotions about it from time to time, but you will realize that deviating from being yourself will only be a setback. Your personality is a great weapon, wield it well because there is a place for you at the table just the way you are. Do not get lost in the melee of things to the point where you lose yourself. Be conscious of the fact that no matter how much of yourself you deny or give up, you are still a woman and sexism will not vanish by adopting other's behaviors. It makes no sense for you to deny yourself only to be oppressed anyway. Be true to yourself, face that oppression and overcome it with your qualities and values intact.

Never stop trying
"Don't let the bastards grind you down." - Margaret Atwood

You must be realistic about your journey from the beginning. This is another important piece of advice; getting the results that you want is not going to be enough. When you get the results, you must keep working hard to keep those results working. You cannot expect good work to automatically get you noticed as a candidate for promotion. You also need to network and package yourselves as a potential CEO. Connect with high-up executives and board members; seek mentors and advocates, and act as a leader with team members and subordinates. Show that you have the ability to take up the reigns when they fall into your hands.

Nothing is perfect all the times, you need to expect that on occasion, a mishap will arise. It will be how you decide to address that situation that others will observe and critique you on. A major key here is to remain approachable and flexible. Allow people the chance to talk to you and be honest and tactful when you hear them out.

People will look at you as a person they can trust and count on if you show you have an advocate's spirit. There will be some people who need a little more push or understanding in order to evolve into the best versions of themselves. You want to be the person they can seek out and learn from because it will make you stand out among the crowd.

Don't Hesitate to Ask
"In politics, if you want anything said, ask a man. If you want anything done, ask a woman." - Margaret Thatcher

Open your mind and accept that there are many opportunities that exist to obtain a role in the C-Suite, but many women are unaware of them because they do not ask. Women are often afraid or reluctant to voice their views. You must pursue them; consider yourself as already being a leader and do not waste time and do not hesitate to ask for what you need to get the job done. It is critical for women to understand the importance of developing this trait as they move forward towards the position of CEO.

When you aspire to become greater than you are, you must be ready to make serious changes. This starts with acknowledging your ambitions and seeing yourself as a leader. You will need to accept work-life compromises and make negotiations within them. You will also likely need to toughen up to overcome both internal and external barriers.

You might find that even after you have reached the executive role that you are lacking the support and authority needed to accomplish specific strategies and goals. This is one of the leading reasons many female leaders have shorter tenures than their male counterparts. To overcome this barrier female CEOs must creating self-development programs instead of subscribing to the formal developmental programs that are male-dominated. Many women still feel they live in a man's world and the market is tailored for men, so as a female CEO or an aspiring female CEO, you should develop your strategy to self-educate and polish your skill sets. Venture out and find loopholes; one such method is to actively develop network connections that help your career and to seek out your own mentors. Do not rely on the same methods that are used by others because they may not work the same way for you.

Always take active ownership of your own life, career, and the opportunities available to you. This is crucial for female leadership careers as these are the defining factors in who will become a female leader – and who does not. The difficult work-life trade-offs are faced by all leaders, but there are other factors you will face as a woman. Women often encounter excessive criticism for prioritizing their career over their families and children, especially from those who still endorse traditional gender roles. As a female CEO, you must realize that prioritizing your own development over that of others—especially your families—requires a particularly self-accepting and effortful choice for what you will become, what you will give up, and the criticisms you will face. Fight for what you want and believe that you deserve it. Ask for the opportunities you need to become successful and do not shy away from any chance that comes your way. Become the things that leaders are made of and you can become a spectacular leader. But you will need to go out of your way and push yourself out of your comfort zone.

Chapter 3: Promote Yourself

"I could not, at any age, be content to take my place by the fireside and simply look on. Life was meant to be lived. Curiosity must be kept alive. One must never, for whatever reason, turn his back on life." - Eleanor Roosevelt

Women excel at working hard, keeping their heads down, and being productive at their jobs. As positive as this sounds, it may not be the most effective method for them to achieve your goals. It is great to work hard, that is how the job should be done but try to lift your chin a bit. After a job well done, firms tend to look and take notice, if you have stuck your head in the sand, they will overlook your contribution completely. You want them to see you and know that you are the person behind the masterpiece. Take credit for the work you did; it is completely right to do so.

You must promote yourself in your own workspace. According to a report by LeanIn.Org and McKinsey &

Company in 2018, women face a challenge when it comes to promotion to leadership roles. This happens even though the number of women in the workforce have higher academic qualifications than men. The report shows that men hold 62% of managerial seats while women hold only 38%. In the same survey, 24% of women and 8% of men interviewed admitted that promotion in companies is biased with men always taking the greater share (Zipkin 2018).

Here are a few key pointers on how to promote yourself successfully:

- Talk about your team's success – this will help them to see your leadership potential.

- It is important to do networking both inside and outside of your company.

- Define your targets and the people you want to promote yourself to. When selecting targets, include everyone within your company and outside of it.

- Keep it short. People do not enjoy listening to a 35-minute pitch that is about nothing more than how you just completed your most recent assignment. Nobody enjoys a boring lecture.

In order to earn admiration, you must first deliver the goods. You don't get the right to boast until you have put in the hard work and proven yourself. Make sure that the accomplishments you share are relevant and that you have real facts and success to share.

Many women are modest about the success they have achieved throughout their life. This is a setback and a mindset to overcome. You should not be afraid to share your accomplishments. Some women are afraid it would make them appear vain or conceited. Therefore, they are not quick to self-promote, but it is important to remember that there is absolutely nothing wrong with the acknowledgment of your success. Learn the difference between what is honest promotion and shameless bragging. There is a huge difference in bragging and sharing. You should never assume that others know what you have achieved. Sharing your story with others can encourage other women to come forth and share their stories. This will help you build a network and before you know it, there will be hidden talent surfacing everywhere, eager to support you. The sad fact is, most women doubt the talents they already have, and this causes them to shy away from their own success. Start thinking of strategies to promote yourself.

Remember, you cannot expect to progress and climb the ladder simply by doing a good job alone. You must promote yourself. This will definitely push many women out of their comfort zones but it is necessary. Today you can promote yourself in many ways. Build a support group around you, people that will encourage you to strive for more, don't shy away anymore, it is your time to shine. You can do this on a weekly or monthly basis. Don't just talk about yourself, but about each other as well. This also helps other women who may experience some self-esteem issues. Discuss the accomplishments reached throughout the month and set up new goals for the next month. This group will also help you focus on your value in the company, and to remind others of their value as well. The idea is that you are simply letting your work come out of hiding and letting it promote itself. Do not talk about unnecessary things like the extra hours that you have put into a project because that will turn into bragging. You must be comfortable with sharing your accomplishments with others, but not too comfortable. The key here is presenting it in a professional manner. Your success in your career will ultimately depend on how well you can promote yourself.

Whatever you do, do not block other female employees, back them up. You'll see that in time they will do the same for you. There is a natural inclination towards competition in business, but don't let that tendency affect you.

An important thing to always keep in mind is your connections. Think about your group on social media, get professional people in your circle and share some of your ideas (i.e. Business Marketing Strategies). Let people see what talent grows inside of you. Not only will they see you as a talented person in life, but they will also see you as a corporate asset to their company. Thus, you have proven to people without overdoing it or being too direct about it. Think of clever ways to boost yourself in every way possible.

Having enough confidence to promote yourself will help you to become visible. Know that your confidence goes hand-in-hand with your self-esteem. If there is a low self-esteem problem, look within yourself to try to solve it. Fixing the problem is easier than you think; try to adopt a confident mindset (it is surprising how powerful the mind can be).

If there is a promotion coming up, some women may tend not to apply for the promotion because they feel they do not fit all the needed requirements. There might be qualifications that are listed that you don't have, but you never know exactly what they are looking for and you can make up for those in other ways. So don't let it slip away. Talk to the hiring manager about the requirements that are not met. Take the chance the next time a promotion comes up.

Be prepared to say yes to responsibility
"Owning our story can be hard but not nearly as difficult as spending our lives running from it." - Brene Brown

Though there are many women well on their way to becoming CEOs, many express that they are not ready for success. This can be a huge turnoff for prospective partners because they need someone who is ready to call the long shots before they ever get the authority to do so. Once you become a larger part of an organization, you work hard and you volunteer to take on the responsibilities that nobody else wants, then you are already working toward the top spot. You may as well be prepared to say yes when the question you have been patiently waiting to be asked is finally asked.

Remind yourself that the fact that the organization has decided to put sexism aside and invite you to sit at the table is an indicator that they think you are ready. Don´t miss the opportunity because it may not come again even if you move mountains. You must be prepared to say yes and assume the authority you are given once the opportunity presents itself. Becoming a female CEO is difficult in a world where sexism is such a potent form of oppression, but if you prove to be phenomenal, you are arming yourself to be successful despite it.

Boosting your confidence
"You have to have confidence in your ability, and then be tough enough to follow through." - Rosalynn Carter

Do not be afraid to push yourself and take risks, whether it is for personal development or in the workspace. We all know that risks are inevitable, if you don't risk it, someone else will. One of the reasons men tend to advance faster because they are willing to take more risks, like applying for a promotion even if they only meet a portion of the requirements. Don't be afraid to take risks because sometimes risks pay off and end up being a huge success and even if they do not, there will always be a next time and a learning opportunity. Here are a few tips to prepare you to take those risk:

Prepare to be confident (yes, you must actually prepare yourself for that). It is important that you take time to prepare and to plan for the situations that your most nervous about. Also, try to identify a "trigger" that brings out that confident version of you and use that trigger when you need a bit of a confidence boost.

Know and understand. Nothing inspires confidence like planning. B knowing your material and being an expert on a specific subject, you will be more likely to have confidence flowing through you. Grab and seize every opportunity so you can boost your expertise.

Fear must not stop you. We all know that no one wants to fail but seeing failure for what it truly is can help. All it is, is a minor setback from which you can learn a valuable lesson and adapt. It happens to everyone, even corporate leaders. The experience itself can be a confidence booster once you have overcome this mental block.

Positive attitude adjustments. Positive people attract positive things. If you have the right attitude, you can achieve any goal you focus on. It is important to surrounded yourself with other confident people; not only will it become easier to be confident, but you can learn pointers from them.

Learn to say no and be comfortable with the outcome. It may be a very short word, but most women struggle to say it, because we all know that people do not want to hear it. We strive to keep people happy and that is why we are tempted to withhold it.

Taking smart risks
"Courageous risks are life-giving, they help you grow, make you brave, and better than you think you are." - Joan L. Curcio

Taking a risk may show your superiors you are bold, that you are not afraid. Failure is not a bad thing, nor is it lasting. It gives you a chance to learn, grow and make future attempts to do better. Show your superiors that you are paying attention and that you know exactly what you are doing. Stay motivated enough or you will find yourself dwelling on the misery of missing an opportunity.

Sometimes there are executives who want to see a certain "trait" in you before considering you for a promotion. People who stay stuck in their role are a gamble when considering candidates for promotion. Take a step outside of your responsibilities because it will show that you have potential skills to go further. When you are willing to own additional responsibilities and delegate some to others on your team, you will be given a second look.

- Think outside the box to change the company for the better.

- Thinking in terms of helping the company instead of just in terms of your job shows that you can think independently.

- Even the simplest things such as being punctual will get you noticed because it shows you possess work ethics.

Always try to take that one step further and use your initiative. Try expanding your knowledge and expertise. When you set up goals and work hard to reach them, it will show you are dependable and that will make you stand out from the crowd.

The most important thing to keep in mind when it comes to empowering yourself in any workplace is that no matter what your career is, you must define your goals clearly and internalize what you wish to achieve. There are many factors to consider whenever you set up goals for yourself, some you will have control over and others you will not. Always have a back-up plan for when those factors you don't have control over fail. You must not make goals for yourself that are too complicated, make your goals clear. Remember that your plans must have flexibility, you can adapt your goals, keeping your priorities in mind. You can achieve goals faster and easier with help. Two of the most commonly required soft skills nowadays are flexibility and teamwork.

Write your goals down so you can see your goals every day. Tick them off as you go along, whether they are long-term or short-term. You'll find that you will feel you have accomplished so much more. Keep track of your accomplishments; it may be difficult to recall your success in the past, but as time goes on it will get easier. This will also inspire your future goals, especially in the tough times.

Developing self-worth

"A strong woman understands that the gifts such as logic, decisiveness, and strength are just as feminine as intuition and emotional connection. She values and uses all of her gifts." - Nancy Rathburn

Your sense of self-worth plays a vital role in the ability to push yourself forward in the workplace. Know that you have a right to make your own choices, don't let anyone choose for you. Just as importantly, don't let your lack of making choices be your downfall. Seize every opportunity you can. For example, whether you are doing solo or team assignments, know that your input is important. Understand that you are important and worthy enough to have been included. There is an increasing number of women leaders for a reason. By making more gender equalizing investments, we are bringing a brighter future not just to the company but to the world.

As more female role models get noticed and established in the workplace, the goal of women getting to the top will be more and more attainable. Show others the way and encourage them to get there. Role models can inspire women to strive further and bring them out of their shells; this is the fastest and often the easier method of developing self-worth. It is critical that you find your own female role models, identify yourself with those role models, and don't be afraid to internalize their advice. It is worth taking the time to celebrate the women who have faced similar struggles, survived and overcame them. Having a mentor can provide a great amount of help so try to find one within your organization, someone who can help you and provide advice. This mentor should act as your sponsor, as someone who can, in time, help to promote your career. It is invaluable to have a spokesperson who can introduce you to influential people and open doors for you. This is a huge advantage and no matter who the source is, getting positive exposure will only be beneficial for you.

When you take credit for what you bring to the table do not forget to give credit to the other people who have brought tremendous amounts of success to the company as well. While it is great to stand up on your own two feet, you also do not want to push out the opportunity for others to excel. Even though the workplace is typically a competitive market, when you work as a team you must allow everyone a chance to be heard and seen so that nobody feels like they have fallen between the cracks and become invisible.

An important aspect of self-worth is the ability to be resilient, women who have reached CEO status all share this as a common trait. These women became aware of their own barriers and filters. Because everyone sees the world a little differently, the way you develop a thick skin may differ somewhat from others, but there are a few things that stay the same:

- Knowing what upsets and bothers you is key

- Try not to become overly critical of yourself if something happens that you are normally upset by, this is how you will practice controlling your emotions

- Keep in mind that while you cannot control everyone or everything you are in complete control of yourself

People will say things to try to push past your resilience just to see if you will fall apart so they can use that to prove you unfit for your dreams. To combat this, you must become desensitized to their attempts. This does not mean that you should just turn a blind eye when something bad happens, but it means not taking everything said or done as a personal attack, even if it is.

Chapter 4: Be Yourself

"Don't be intimidated by what you don't know. That can be your greatest strength and ensure that you do things differently from everyone else" - Sara Blakely

One of the most defining pieces of career advice today is to focus on being yourself. It's trendy. Everyone recommends it, from college students to CEO's. But how true is it?

Some companies actively encourage employees to be themselves. They want to create a workspace where you can be yourself through various types of self-expression, wanting to lift the barriers that would stop a person from fully embracing who they are. Employees in these types of organizations are often challenged to use their creativity to explore new ideas that will help the organization to grow, no matter what the employees' background or experiences are. If an employee demonstrates a better idea or way of doing something, they are empowered by management rather than discouraged. These types of organization are rare and there are often trade-offs when working for them; but great organizations are out there, so don't settle for too long.

In most organizations, women face different problems than men in their workspaces, some of these can prevent you from embracing who you are. One of these challenges in finding work-life balance. Work-life balance sounds easier than it is. Finding a healthy balance between personal life and work life is critical; this means knowing where to draw the line between work and home. You must make sure that your priorities are sorted out, not just your personal ones, but your professional ones as well. Be honest and open with your superiors and employees when a situation comes up in life, like when your child or spouse is sick, this is a part of who you are. Admitting that you cannot do everything on your own is not a weakness and there are alternative solutions that won't affect your performance. Perhaps you can allow your spouse to make dinner in the evening if you must stay late at work to meet a deadline. If you know that you are no longer needed at the office, though, maybe take the time to go pick up something nice for takeout and bring it back to spend more time with your family.

Finding a work-life balance that works for you is a critical step that will require some introspection. It is a sliding scale, some days the scales will tip in favor of either side of your life. Just work on not allowing either side to push out the other because this is where many women find themselves feeling burnout. Focus on ways to be the best you in everything you do, and you are sure to succeed in finding a modest balance.

Believe in yourself
"I love having every right to be as outspoken as I am, as any man would be." - Chrissy Teigen

Women are often told to believe in themselves as they aspire to seek after their goals and dreams, whether by parents, career counselors, or just people they meet day to day. To the point where it has now become cliché. But the fact that so many people encourage it speaks to both its challenges and its importance. Belief in one's self is of utmost importance; if you have a lack of self-confidence you will not dream of the C-suite, let alone try to enter it. At the cornerstone of every strong leader is an even stronger sense of self-belief. This simple concepts is discussed many times in this book and that is because you will likely need to constantly remind yourself of your talent, your ability to succeed and lead – no matter how few women have attempted to do so in the past. Don´t question if you have the potential to do this because the second you doubt yourself is the second you become unable to do it. Some may find it easier to support the hopes and dreams of others as opposed to supporting and working on their own. The same belief that you have in another individual's hopes and dreams can be transferred to you and you can become the propellant you need.

A serious internal issue faced by women is that they regularly walk away from leadership roles. There may be various reasons to do this, but the fact is that passing up increases in responsibility eliminate the possibility of mission-focused positions that can give your career an advantage. Remember that you might not succeed every time, but with focus and practice you will succeed. Don´t let a small failure keep you from ever trying again. If you don't experience failure, you can't learn the valuable lessons that will help in the future. Rather be graceful about failure and do not give up. The key here is to get back up again.

Because of long-held beliefs and cultural influences, women may be incudes to shy away when they notice they may be the only woman among many men at higher levels. However, it is a mistake to keep quiet; do not put on the silent act. Stand up and make your voice heard. Understand that you should play an active role; if you do that, soon enough you will find that you own your position. So, rise, speak volumes. Lift your hand up in the meetings, give your suggestions, and you will see that those around you will lift you even higher. They will see you as a member, not just as a woman.

There will be times when you will find that you, are your greatest challenge. This is because you are the one who pushes yourself the hardest. You expect the most from yourself. As an aspiring CEO, women need to push themselves constantly. Have a chat with yourself, quiz, and challenge yourself about the plans, dreams, and aspirations that you have as an individual. By doing this you might find yourself asking very interesting and challenging questions which in turn may help you realize how much you want the position and what needs to be done to prepare.

Since many women are challenged by self-doubt, this is a good way to break yourself free from the chains that you have attached to yourself. Many times, women fail to ask themselves two very crucial questions; what am I good at and what do I want to achieve? As an aspiring CEO, you need to ask yourself these questions and verbalize what you want to accomplish – yes, say it out loud.

We are often so caught up in the detail, trying so hard to be brilliant at what we are doing right now, that we don't take the time to stop and think about our talents, much less talk about ourselves. So, ask yourself hard questions about your true ambitions and be honest with yourself, make sure you know when you are truly ready to take that next step.

Authenticity

"We have to dare to be ourselves, however frightening or strange that self may prove to be." - May Sarton

Authenticity starts with self-awareness. This means that you should know who you are from the inside out. Being yourself can have many different meanings. You can open yourself up a bit more, letting employees see your personal professional struggles, but also your achievements and successes, just remember not to go into too much detail. This brings up another point to consider when you are finally offered a position in the C-suite, there seems to be a growing trend of women being offered CEO positions that other men do not wish to fill. If you are given the opportunity to become a CEO will you take the role just because you are vying after the title or will you take the time to polish yourself to fit into the role of CEO for a company you actually respect and enjoy? Do not take whatever is offered simply because you want to have a title.

Make sure that you are being authentic with yourself and your overall goals before accepting more responsibility just to earn the CEO label. It is important to remember that there is no problem being yourself in the workspace. You just need to remember to keep your professional image polished at all times. Be yourself, but in the workplace, you should always behave with tact and professionalism. This is a balancing act and a critical skill to master.

What can also help you to develop your authenticity is to develop a comfort level with yourself. It can also help you to boost your confidence. It is at this point that you will notice people regarding you with respect and doors will be held open to you, literally and metaphorically. There are advantages that come with being a woman, the first one being the benefit of seeing things differently.

A few tips or "warning signs" that tell you when you are NOT being authentic:

- You feel like are not the person you know you are deep inside. Feeling phony, fraudulent or fake.

- Recognizing that the lifestyle you truly want is not the one you are living.

- Continually choosing to ignore or suppress your intuition.

- You're unnecessarily on edge (being aggressive, protective or argumentative).

- The realism of life feels like somewhat of a struggle.

- When you want to reconnect with yourself, because you cannot.

- When you keep your head down and you don't speak your mind.

- To make yourself look good, you lie and cover up details of a story or embellish.

Empowering yourself
"Women, like men, should try to do the impossible. And when they fail, their failure should be a challenge to others." - Amelia Earhart

Yes, it is true that you should shape and mold yourself to the company culture to excel, but do not change the person you are for a promotion or position. Your inner strengths, your beliefs, it all makes you the person you are. All of those things are what makes you who you are. Eventually, you will see that your unique strengths can help you to climb the ladder to success all the way to the top.

The key to innovation and success in an organization is to have different perspectives readily available. Which supports the concept of employees being themselves, only then can a company truly have diverse perspectives. Tell your colleagues and employers what is important to you, do not be afraid to share your side of the story. Your employer would love to know that you have a life outside of your workplace but keep it professional and polite.

When a woman has been able to fully understand the best time and the best place to be their true selves, she will feel at ease. First, try to find which of your colleagues you feel comfortable with, enough to begin being your true self, start doing this right away. The self-reflective workers are usually the most effective employees, they try to analyze the different situations and their own behaviors. They are the employees who have a big advantage because they often know how to handle any complicated work situations. The trick is to learn that there is a time and place for everything at work, knowing when, where and whom, is solving the puzzle.

People have different behaviors that show who we are at different times. For example, serious or playful, multitasking or focused, quiet or talkative. The trick is to know when which aspect of your personality should be brought forward and is appropriate for the circumstance. Women have the impressive ability to adapt to any given situation.

- Do not do practice the "Alpha Female" concept, there are many different leadership methods, this is not be one of them.

- Make sure that you celebrate the achievements of women in your company, many people don't see something as an achievement until they are celebrated.

- If you see a coworker struggle, reach out to them.

- Find the time to help and give advice to other women in your company, be friendly and accessible.

- Gender equality should reflect on all the work you create.

- Open a discussion when you feel that you have not received the appropriate recognition for your accomplishments, and before you jump to conclusions. Give your colleagues the benefit of the doubt and do not assume they have nefarious or sexist intentions.

- Talk about your "career" and not just your "job" in your working environment.

All of your personality traits (good and bad) which define you should not be hidden, be honest about them. Transparency is important in order to alleviate workspace issues. Discuss things openly to determine strong points and weaknesses. Only from there can you flourish and create a workspace where you can grow.

- Taking notes can also be helpful. Let's face it, there is nothing as frustrating for a boss as when they have to tell you the same thing more than once.

- Keep paper and pen close; we tend to forget mental notes very fast. Technology can be of great help here. Keep your notes handy and this will increase your productivity.

- Don't be afraid to ask your boss if you can help with something, they will appreciate it.

- Always be sure to know what your responsibilities are and make sure you prioritize them.

No one wants to hear when they do something wrong, so let's look at what some potential downfalls are. It may help you if you have not yet noticed them:

- When a specific obstacle stands in your way, express it clearly to the person involved (if there is a specific one, otherwise the whole group). Try to be as transparent as possible and express how you feel.

- When you encounter an unfriendly or unhelpful woman, do not, by any means, feel intimidated. The

"Queen Bee Syndrome" is still very real in the contemporary world workplace. Under no circumstances should you ever feel that you must tolerate this or any similar behaviors. Instead, seek out those who would help to foster growth. Make it known to co-workers and employees, especially those who tend to gossip, that it is unacceptable. There is never a need for anyone to be mean or nasty to others or to create a hostile work environment for the sake of their positions.

- It is important that everyone (male and female) feels comfortable so that they can discuss issues that are specific to women. When you notice that there might be some uneasiness present, address it, treat the discussion with respect.

- When a female colleague has mustered her courage and she finally has come out to talk to you about things that concern her, do not be dismissive. If you do not take this seriously and give it the attention it deserves you will have caused a serious second-guessing issue within that person. Remember that when a woman takes the first step needed to confide in you, your duty is to help ensure them that you appreciate the effort and courage it took to approach you.

It is important for women in management not to see other women as competition, remember that you are all in this together. When we see other women as competition and start "competing" is when most unnecessary mistakes occur, and people step over the line of professionalism.

No matter what it takes to be authentic, know who you are and know how to express yourself in every situation and every moment. That means no hiding who you are, there should be no censoring, but most of all, you should not pretend to be someone else. Do not compare yourself to others, you are unique, do not live up to other people's expectations, have your own. You do not have to defend your reputation from anybody. Just consistently bring out all your good qualities in the workspace and you will be recognized.

Be confident without leaving kindness at the door
"I'm going to do what I want to do. I'm going to be who I really am. I'm going to figure out what that is." - Emma Watson

The line between confidence and arrogance can be incredibly thin, similar to the lines between kindness and submission. Sometimes people confuse those boundaries, and this can lead to a breakdown in communication or even minor arguments. As a woman seeking to enter the C-suite, you must learn the difference in these four things as it will be a defining factor in your success. If you intend on excelling in the workplace, it is important to treat these lines with caution.

Just as we were taught from childhood, manners matter in the boardroom as well. Always be considerate and courteous of others – but never apologize for expressing your opinions and thoughts. Avoid being inconsiderate or rash, do not abuse your power or overstep the boundaries of professionalism. It is difficult to master these attributes, but you can do so by approaching all things with a sense of class and humility.

Some self-discovery may help you understand how you are perceived. One approach for this is to solicit honest feedback from your colleagues, so you can learn about yourself from the eyes of another. This may help you understand what is important for you to focus on and establish areas that you can improve.

Be a compassionate leader, but still a leader
"There is no greater pillar of stability than a strong, free and educated woman. And there is no more inspiring role model than a man who respects and cherishes women and champions their leadership." - Angelina Jolie

The truth of the matter is, running a corporation can be compared to raising children; you cannot be too friendly with your employees, but you must not be cold and distant with them either. Always try to remind yourself that you will never be everybody's friend and that is perfectly okay. Once a relationship is established and all parties work toward the greater good, everything else will fall into place. It is impossible to make everyone happy and it is not necessarily a priority to do so; running the company successfully is.

Keep in mind that you will be under constant observation as an aspiring CEO. This means that even when you aren't feeling your best people will look for confidence and consistency in you as a leader – so if that means giving yourself a pep talk in the mirror or calling a confidante for encouragement, do so and do not let your fears or inhibitions hold you back.

Some key things to remember in this area are that you need to focus on positivity, not negativity. We all have many of our own troubling negative thoughts; however, everyone is looking for a consistent personality of possibility and optimism, that is what you should strive to be.

Consider every word you say and how you are saying it. The way you speak can and will come across differently to other people and they can end up misinterpreting your intentions because of it. You will want to practice this skill because you do not want to develop a monotone voice either. Spend some time speaking with a trusted friend or record yourself and observe your behaviors. If you notice any habits or tones that make you appear unsure or too aggressive, identify and polish these traits.

Keep in mind that team development often fails as a result of trying too hard to form relationships rather than focusing on task relevancy. Next time you are in the middle of a project and you want to share a personal conversation, ask yourself the question of whether it will help you with your work and if it is relevant to the situation. If that is not the case, it would be wise to save the story for a more informal session.

Stay relevant to the task
"Stay on your game and keep going for your dreams. The world needs that special gift that only you have." - Marie Forleo

Focus on generating "positive input" for your organization, depending on your organization, that may be in the form of revenue, new partnerships, clients, customers, etc. Your success is reflected by the generation of positive input for business. If you are generating inputs, you are an asset and that makes you valuable to the company and puts you in a position of power and influence. It´s a fact that generating new positive inputs for your business is a huge difficulty women face when climbing the corporate ladder. Here are some tips to get you started:

- Determine what generates positive input in your organization, no matter what position you are in, and demonstrate an obvious interest in it to other. For example, if you're in Accounting, the positive input might mean getting the monthly reports done on time, or if you in sales it might meeting team's monthly sales quota.

- Always keep a lookout for a loophole or shortcut. This is not about taking immoral or unethical action, this is about intelligently seeking opportunities that exist that haven't yet been identified, you can find these even in the most unlikely of places.

- Seek opportunities to develop experience in profit-and-loss. This is crucial, it shows that you understand this critical function and you will be more apt to notice changes that could affect the company.

An understanding of a profit-and-loss statement goes hand in hand with having the ability to vie for the position of CEO. Any women considering taking on this role must make sure they are thorough in this aspect, as this could be what sets you apart. Being able to handle a profit-and-loss statement is one of the major things that could give you an edge and advantage over your counterparts. Regardless of the fact that you may want to remain modest, it does not take away from the fact that promotion is a competition and you should remain at the top of your game if you plan to outpace others and become the leading choice.

So, what exactly is profit-and-loss statement?

A profit-and-loss statement is a financial statement that summarizes the revenues, costs, and other expenses incurred by a company during a specific period, usually during a fiscal year or quarter. The profit-and-loss statement goes hand in hand with the income statement, which is another important record. These records provide information about whether a company is able to generate profit by increasing revenue, reducing costs or by doing both. It is imperative that the head of a company can understand these documents and unfortunately, many women lack in this experience. For some, this is because they believe they are "not good with numbers" or they just aren't familiar with managing a budget or other financial statements. This is not something that women have been exposed to historically, which makes this function even more crucial for you to master.

Historically, it was difficult for women to gain practical experience with these kinds of reports. If you take some time to ask other women in the workplace about their experiences, you will find that many of them have stories in which they were pushed aside, put down, and told that they did not belong at the table. Some women still never get to sit at the table because they are labeled or deemed inadequate. This is a common experience, but building your education in this area will help you to get past it.

Avoid overly personal disclosures
"There was a moment when I changed from an amateur to a professional. I assumed the burden of a profession, which is to write even when you don't want to, don't much like what you're writing, and aren't writing particularly well." - Agatha Christie, An Autobiography

The disclosure of personal information is often a cultural norm. However, to ensure you retain your professionalism, keep your personal stories away from the work environment, unless they will provide some insight for the team or a certain task your team is working on. When you do share personal information, be sure you are disclosing appropriate information based on your audience. You can look for any clues, such as eye contact, when sharing specific stories; test the waters when attempting this with task-relevant self-disclosure and see how people react to it.

Personal stories can help establish and strengthen relationships, but it requires a delicate balance. If you share too much personal information too quickly, it can break the sociocultural norms of behavior. The psychological affect is that it makes you look unstable in the eyes of others; at best you may come across as awkward. To meet social expectation in the workplace, you must build on topics that are common and first demonstrate credibility. With practice, you will learn when it is helpful to share, and when it is not the right thing to do.

The balance between "being yourself" and limiting personal disclosure can be a complex principle and can be frightening for some people. Achieving confidence in this skill, and yes, it is a skill, will not happen overnight. If you find it difficult to bring out the authentic you in the office, try to start with small steps, not everyone is the same, take the time you need, do not rush this. Be ready to accept your differences rather than hiding them, know that you are taking steps in the right direction.

Be honest in all situations and accept that you are not perfect. It is not always easy to be honest, it takes a lot of work and energy, it's not always the natural thing to do, but it is worth it. This does not mean that you should "wear your heart on your sleeve", but you are human and imperfect. Do not put too much pressure on yourself. When you fail, discuss with others about the things that worked and things that didn't; it's a learning opportunity. Remember to support others in both their successes and failures.

If you are seeking promotion, one of the biggest mistakes you can make is trying to achieve perfection. Not just as a woman in the workspace, but also as a mother, or as a wife, as a friend, etc. Assessing yourself against other women is not healthy, you should only strive to improve yourself. Let go of the "compare and despair" notion. You limit your options by avoiding the need to take risks; being an optimist pays off.

When you work hard to make sure that things run as smoothly as possible, you will not have the time to dwell on what might go wrong. You must be brave because sometimes you will fail, but you will achieve great things as time goes on. If you hold on to the fear that you will fail, it will hold you back from moving forward.

Personal awareness serves a very important role in the work environment. You should try to start your day by setting good intentions, meaning, reminding yourself of your power, the unique gifts you bring, and your strengths. Then, end your day with reflection, summarize your day and identify what you have achieved for the day. Always strive to improve; being a leader means constantly growing. Learn how to do it well, remember it is never too soon or too late to start.

Your relationship with employees

"Ninety percent of leadership is the ability to communicate something people want." - Dianne Feinstein

Employee engagement is critical to the success of a manager and an organizations. Gallup data shows that employees who work for a female manager are engaged for at least 38% for the workday compared to male managers whose employee engagement is only 26%. This percentage reduces further to below 20% where male workers report to male managers. Based on the statistics, for optimal output, female employees work best with female managers to produce a daily work concentration of about 48% (AGRAWAL 2014).

Building productive relationships with employees is the most effective way to increase employee engagement. Treat your team as you would want them to treat key customers. Just because you are their leader does not mean that you have earned a free pass to indulge your baser instincts. You should try to find ways to support your team and to help them become successful, rather than to be servile. Always ask yourself what you can do to help them succeed, rather than how they can help you to look good. Once you are thinking about your employees' satisfaction, you have already taken the most difficult step that many managers stumble on. Treating your employees as if they are internal customers is a great approach to establishing your role without being too demanding. Implement this approach with technology, your employees should be able to access critical information at any time. That way you make them accustomed to the interactive self-service options available to them. When they can then find information on their own, it will help them grow and develop skills. It is also a happy side effect that employees become more productive and loyal to the company.

As a leader, care about your employees as real people, treating them with respect and the understanding that there are important needs outside the office, just as there are inside. You will know you have succeeded as a leader when you see that your employees care about you as a person. Leaders should always keep in mind that employees spend more than half their waking lives at work, so why not try to make it a pleasant experience? Employees give their best when you consistently treat them with respect, dignity, and trust. If you want to get the best out of your employees, remember to treat them like your most loyal customers.

Do not be afraid to shape and mold your employees so they can become the best that they can be. This will not just be a benefit to them, but to you as a leader as well.

- Teach them accountability - they must be reliable, they must know their duties, they must be responsible.

- Teach them commitment, they must also know where their obligations lay and how to keep their promises.

- Encourage them to self-educate. Continuous learning will result in improvement over time.

- Empowerment is key - Taking initiative will make them self-sufficient and improve their drive.

- Teach them to be approachable, willing to answer questions and able to accept consequences for both action and inaction. They must also know how to graciously accept credit for the work they do.

Sometimes it is better to ask for feedback from your team, rather than to wait for it. Do not wait for your employees offer feedback to you. They might never feel brave enough to do so, and you'll be missing what might have been a very valuable opportunity for feedback for you and your company. You miss an opportunity to learn when you take unsolicited feedback the wrong way (seeing it as criticism).

A good leader must also know how to earn their employees' trust. Use these steps to help earn your teams' trust:

- Always treat your team with respect. If you show them you are honest with what you feel, they will trust you. When showing compassion, it must come from the heart; they will be able to tell when you are genuine.

- Don't ever use inappropriate language, it will make them feel unsafe and insecure.

- Try to hear them out when they are expressing their opinions and remember to praise them when they have done good work. There is nothing wrong with showing them you are proud of them.

- You are an example in your workspace, so remember that your team will follow the model you set to be. Be on your best behavior and so they will.

Keeping your promises is a key feature in building trust with your team. You will lose the respect and trust when you break promises or fail to keep your word.

Knowing what you can and cannot do will help you keep your trustworthiness. Remember to be realistic and make sure you can deliver before making any promises.

You are the leader, there is only one person you can hold accountable; that person is you. You must remember that you are the person who makes decisions, so stand by them. You are also the only person who will be responsible for the consequences. Do not blame your team for the mistakes you have made, they are not a cover for you. You now have a role that includes ownership, know that you are responsible for everything. By being the "captain" of your ship, the fate of your ship can only lay in your hands, steer it in the right direction and keep it safe.

For things to run smoothly, make sure you delegate tasks and roles clearly to your team. Give every team member clear expectation of what you want. Micromanaging your team or to trying to do everything yourself is not the way to go. When there is training involved and you must train someone, demonstrate the task as detailed as you can and narrate all the steps as you do them. You can then observe them as they do the task, if possible, to give you more peace of mind. When they make errors, gently correct them. If you set your team up for success, you will also find that it is easier to trust them.

At work, make sure you listen to your employees with an active mind. When you talk, make sure you explain things clearly to them. As a leader who is balanced, the environment you create must be fair to everyone that is part of it.

Chapter 5: Package yourself as a leader

"Women are leaders everywhere you look — from the CEO who runs a Fortune 500 company to the housewife who raises her children and heads her household. Our country was built by strong women, and we will continue to break down walls and defy stereotypes." - Nancy Pelosi

Leadership qualities and skills are not something you are born with. You grow the ability gradually and at different stages in your life. The attitudes you have in certain situations and the conscious reflections upon them will show yourself, and others that you are ready to be a leader.

The first and most important thing you can do to package yourself as a successful leader is to work on your mindset. Start to understand and accept yourself and how you fit into the organization in order to advance to any desired leadership position. Here are the most fundamental steps you can take to understand yourself and your role in the organization:

- ✓ **We vs. Me**

In a leadership role, it is critical that you cannot maintain a mindset of viewing your employees and their output as separate from you. That is not the mind of a leader. Yes, you are their boss, but you are also their colleague. You know that you work for the same company, so you share the same goals. The truth is that you have a lot more in common than you might think. Remember that you are very important to them and their participation and acceptance will be a much bigger motivator than fear. Fear can be used effectively, but the risk is rarely worth the benefit, go one step too far and you'll find that no one will want to work with you, and you will lose the team you spent so much time building.

- ✓ **Now vs. Later**

Most leaders today are looking at what people can bring to the table and how they can influence a company. They want to weigh how an employee can become an "asset" to their company vs the value they may already have. The most important thing that sets a leader apart is long-term commitment. A boss will be concerned with meeting the monthly target; a leader will understand the value of the team and focus on development which will lead to a future where they will always be on target. It is true that trying to be a leader is difficult, but by being understanding you can learn a lot.

✓ Use vs. Develop

People are not tools; you cannot wait and see what is being handed to you or what comes your way in your working environment. By trying to do so you are mimicking the past and likely repeating what has already been done. This is not a good strategy; it does not make you different or help you to stand out as a potential leader. Your personal development is up to you. To make progress in your work you have to grab every opportunity that presents itself. A great way to expand employees' range of skills is to offer training or classes. It will also make them feel that they have accomplished more and are valued, even without a promotion.

✓ Fear vs. Respect

Everyone knows the type of boss that just wants to intimidate other people, you may have even experienced it once or twice throughout your life. We know that when you use fear in the right way, it can prove to be in your favor. Use it the wrong way, you will end up with high turnover and a very strained working environment. Respect is be a better motivator in the long run and is a much better tool than fear. When employees are frightened by you, their mindset naturally turns against you, where if they have respect for you and you allow then to be authentic, they will work harder and be happier versions of themselves. Respect goes much further than fear in the long run.

When you have respect in your company, employees will last longer and there will be open and honest communication.

✓ Indifference vs. Empathy

It's an unfortunate fact that there are employees you can classify as "flakes", it's just a fact of management, and there are those employees that do not want to work. But sometimes there are people that really want to work and try to put in effort, but there is something that prevents them from doing so.

For every employee to do their best, personally or professionally, the key lies in a manager hat can meet their needs. A leader must occasionally put themselves in the shoes of their employees to understand, this can have a dramatic impact on employees. In this case, it is not necessarily the effect of the effort you make, what really matters is that you made the effort to understand.

Being a true leader

"Leadership is not a person or a position. It is a complex moral relationship between people based on trust, obligation, commitment, emotion, and a shared vision of the good." - Joanne Ciulla

Being a leader is not just about the fact that you are controlling people. To lead others you must first be able to lead yourself consistently. This is a very important trait you must master before taking any further steps. How can you lead anyone if you have no direction yourself? You will surely lead your followers into a dead-end or off a cliff if you have no road map to get to where you are going. Improve yourself as a leader and take the time to find the ability to direct yourself. This will be the foundation you build for yourself as you work toward becoming a better leader. As simple as it seems, there is absolutely no way you will successfully lead anyone else if you cannot follow and meet your own goals. Good leaders must be self-disciplined and intentional with their actions, but most of all, they must be self-aware of who they truly are as an individual.

To be an effective leader, you must always keep the promises you make. Do not make promises if you are not sure you can keep them. Not keeping a promise instantly kills your credibility. By keeping our commitments we prove our value as a leader and though it may be difficult at times, this is an important way to earn respect. Integrity is one of the greatest tools good leaders can equip themselves with. It may be easier when you make fewer and better commitments. Always track your primary commitments. Having a large number of commitments can cause a leader to become overwhelmed and not be able to fulfill all of them. Track of your commitments with a pen and notepad or use the software on a computer, or an app on your smartphone. There are many creative ways to keep track of commitment, just remember to do it in such a manner that you will see it and be reminded of your commitments on a regular basis.

Don't be afraid to ask for commitments from others. Another mistake often made by leaders is not articulating clear enough what the commitment is that they are asking for. Keep it simple and perhaps show your team how they can get started fulfilling the request. It will surprise you how much easier employees find the request. Another way to help your employees to deliver on their promises is to invest in repeatable processes. Any new leader must also be aware of what previous commitments were made before they stepped in. If you don't, you risk increasing the chance of resistance, as well as undermining trust without knowing that you are violating prior commitments. Make sure that prior commitments are kept or adjusted, don't be afraid to ask what those previous commitments were and find ways to reach them, if possible.

Leaders often focus only on what they "own", not on connecting with other groups. Connect other departments to each other so they see what your common goals are. These connections help can assist with the end-result and impact your company in great ways. You can make sure teams understand how they should work together in order to help the business succeed and by ensuring that your company's goals are being met. Make sure employees know their priorities and understand the goals that you have set.

Education & experience

"There is no end to education. It is not that you read a book, pass an examination, and finish with education. The whole of life, from the moment you are born to the moment you die, is a process of learning." - Jiddu Krishnamurti

Some people make their career choices based on the path that their parents took or that family members wished for them to take. Sometimes career choices are selected based on what a role entails or because of a role model's influence. This tendency sheds some light on why some women choose the career paths they do. You will find many women choosing educational or medical roles that will land them a blossoming career in the fields of teaching, nursing, or possibly scientists or doctors. You will find a great majority of women focusing on subjects from the sciences, arts and on rare occasion, economics. Later on in life, when they become confident enough to strive to climb the corporate ladder they realize they may have to go back and spend years in school to become qualified to take on the role that they now have their eyes set on. Any woman who desires to become a leading member in the business community should take a certain educational path that will allow them to focus on the subjects of business, legal, accounting and economics.

To become CEO, a degree in one of these areas may help, but it is not necessarily a requirement. Studies in these areas provide evidence that the individual can focus and apply appropriate effort to an endeavor. However, the truth of the matter is no one really cares about a liberal arts degree, or other generic degrees; they are likely not worth the effort in the business world. If you aim to enter the C-suite in your lifetime, it will be to your benefit to ensure that you get the fundamentals lined up, and the easiest way is with the appropriate courses of study.

Education gives you an advantage over others and it raises your earning potential. Education alone might not empower women, but it allows them access to a broad range of possibilities. In the previous chapter, we discussed profit-and-loss statements is a common hurdle for women when climbing the corporate ladder. An education is business, accounting or economics can provide this beneficial background.

A large portion of female CEOs who have degrees in Business, Engineering, Technology or Mathematics express that this has helped them prove their ability to take on a traditionally male-dominated area. If you want to be different, you must first realize that your background studies need to be different. Customize your education to be a balance of both STEM-focused subjects and subjects to become self-sufficient and resourceful in a corporate atmosphere.

Let's continue to move away from what women are usually encouraged to do and look at what really matters. Studies in the areas of business, math, technology, and economics will most likely be the areas that will help with the basic knowledge needed to understand and run a company. However, having an MBA will help with qualification and where the qualification comes from rarely makes a difference in most organizations.

There are many women who are CEOs right now who did not start out with a degree from a prestigious college. Having a degree from an Ivy League school could give you an edge, however, it is not necessary. Most female CEO´s who have degrees from an Ivy League college did not necessarily do so because they aspired to be CEOs, but because they all came from prominent families that made sure they received this sort of education. If having a predetermined set of qualifications was required to be a CEO, there would be far fewer men who could qualify to become CEO without first having to go back to school and relive their entire college experience.

Working toward the C-Suite
"I have chosen to no longer be apologetic for my femininity. And I want to be respected in all my femaleness. Because I deserve to be." - Chimamanda Ngozi Adichie

You are already halfway to becoming a CEO, even though you may not think so. You should trace your life all the way back to when you were a child, especially if you have siblings, and you will see evidence. You probably had to learn to ask for things and make your presence known from an early age. Undoubtedly, you probably had to negotiate with your parents for the right to do things that only your siblings were privileged with or allowed to do. The truth is, too many women, especially those who work in male-dominated fields believe that landing a job as a CEO is just a silly dream and completely out of their reach. It is not.

Many women who have moved up the corporate ladder thought they could never become CEO until someone else mentioned it to them, or the opportunity presented itself. Many of them did not even realize it was something they could aspire to do or even work towards and because they truly believed it to be out of their grasp, they never put in the effort to go for it on their own. Every day there are talented women who work hard, pushing themselves to the max and riding head to head with the "big boys" and even though they see that they are more than good enough, they still take a back seat, biting their tongues and second-guessing their ideas – no matter how brilliant they may be. This is your turning point; today women make up 47% of the workforce and there is no reason they cannot hold the equivalent number of top executive roles. Realize that you need to be proactive from the moment you realized that you want to see your name followed by the coveted title of 'CEO.'

Prepare more than you have to
"If you just set out to be liked, you would be prepared to compromise on anything at any time, and you would achieve nothing." - Margaret Thatcher

Having the ability to walk into a conference room filled with men in suits can be very intimidating. You may even get the notion of feeling inexperienced, but you can get over that by simply being over-prepared for the day.

- Do your research ahead of time. Learn everything about the topic(s) being discussed. Practice speaking on the topic in private or with a loved one, so you are knowledgeable, articulate and comfortable with the subject.

- Anticipate the next steps. Look forward to seeing what lies ahead and be prepared for those steps. Be ready for the next move well before it presents itself to you.

- Walk in with an agenda — have a list of questions ready and your ideas around the topic at hand so that you will be miles ahead of the curve and ready for whatever might pop-up unexpectedly. Having a plan of action in place ahead of time prevents mistakes and insecurity from rearing their ugly heads during critical meetings.

Once you walk in looking like you are all about business you will exude this attitude, earning the respect of your male counterparts and putting aside any doubts that they might have about you. There will have been doubts that might not necessarily stem from the fact that you are unqualified, but simply exist because your male peers are not accustomed to having a woman at the helm.

While you are preparing for your dream job there are a couple of other things that you can do to make sure that your transition is right on track:

- Start having meetings with key people. Network with the people you need to impress and discuss important issues and topics with those people.

- Take another look at the business or project structure and outline areas that you feel could be improved upon. You can absolutely begin to impact your company starting from day one by looking ahead and doing your due diligence. Think of it like homework; the reason homework is given to you is to provide you with an opportunity to show your abilities. In this setting, this will bring a sense of assurance to your teammates.

- Maintain a consistent habit of keeping yourself in "the know." In other words, know your role, expectations and the things needed to qualify for your job. After you have come educationally prepared you must then know the position functions and what is expected of you so you can make sure you fulfill those expectations successfully.

- Never forget that only your best is good enough, you may not be able to please everyone, but do try to please the majority and take the time to put maximum effort into everything you do.

There is absolutely no shame in delegating tasks if the workload becomes overwhelming, no person is an island, but try your best to do your job as much as possible and take accountability and ownership of your responsibilities.

Bring something different to the table
"I've come to believe that each of us has a personal calling that's as unique as a fingerprint – and that the best way to succeed is to discover what you love and then find a way to offer it to others in the form of service, working hard, and also allowing the energy of the universe to lead you." - Oprah Winfrey

Everyone likes to see, hear or experience something new; some people will go out of their way to find it. New things attract attention. Try to consider this fact when being the only woman in a room. It can be an opportunity rather than a challenge; a blessing instead of a curse if you look at it from the right point of view. Being a female CEO is not normal (yet) and because of that you already have everyone's attention, so stay focused on keeping it. Women tend to offer fresh perspectives, different insights and an intuition that most men cannot mimic. Seize these advantages and utilize them.

Reinforce what makes you different and capitalize on that. For example, there may have been certain things that needed to be done, but maybe you did not yet have the authority to accomplish them. Now is the time to act on those objectives. Just remember to keep yourself in check and ensure that your intentions are pure and that you are not pushing personal agendas.

Endeavor to come to every meeting fully prepared and armed with a 'unique gift' – be that an insight or an idea – that will add value to the discussion and challenge other members of the board to do the same.

Playing the Long Game
"Women don't take enough risks. Men are just 'foot on the gas pedal.' We're not going to close the achievement gap until we close the ambition gap." - Sheryl Sandberg

The climb to CEO is usually long and tedious. As if taking on the challenge isn't hard enough, you must consider the criticisms that woman who choose career over the family face. As was established earlier, there is a specific role that women are expected to play in society. If a woman for any reason decides this is not enough for her and chooses to walk down a different path, society looks down their noses at her. This makes it twice as hard, so as an aspiring CEO, you must be ready to go for the long haul and stick to the plan.

In the not-so-distant past, women could not sit for certain subjects in school that would give them the education they needed to compete in a male-saturated work environment. Even today, when a woman starts high school or college, she is typically guided towards the liberal arts, and sometimes the sciences because, in the back of most people's minds, women are natural born caregivers and those subject areas will lead them down the path to becoming teachers, nurses or nurse aides or doctors. If they, for any reason, decide that they want to shake things up a little and take on different subjects they are sometimes met with oppression, today that oppression is social and indirect. But the question is; would people be more supportive of women taking on these lessons if they are made aware that you have chosen this educational path because you are working your way into the C-suite or would it still be met with the same amount of resistance?

Because of societal resistance, women do not transition into the CEO role as easily as the men do. For a woman to take over as CEO at a Fortune Five Hundred company she usually has to have years of successful service under her belt and sometimes has to have friends in very high places.

Those select women who become successful CEOs have all faced this. It is difficult to theorize about what drives the long-tenure or why exactly their experiences differ from their male counterparts. One could be optimistic and lend their success to being surrounded by good people and having a network of people who encouraged them. Optimistic interpretations could include supportive organizations, strong mentors, or something intrinsic to the women themselves. It is hard to say because it is an individual journey, but you might find that the latter outweighs the former. On the other hand, the differences between the long stints for women and men could result from the structures that treat women less favorably such as biases that delay promotions or penalties for taking maternity leave. Whatever the root cause of it may be, it is important to acknowledge that the long climb is the common path for female CEOs.

Confidence & Power

"The size of your dreams must always exceed your current capacity to achieve them. If your dreams do not scare you, they are not big enough."- Ellen Johnson Sirleaf

From a mile away, you can see a person with confidence. Confidence will be one of your biggest tools as a leader. Strive to exude confidence even when you do not know all the answers. Here are a few quick tips on how to do that:

- Keep good eye contact

- Maintain a strong posture

- Gesture when you talk to highlight your main key points

- Have faith in your ability to help your employees get from one point to another

Be secure enough to admit when you don't know something. But do it carefully, when you don't know something, don't say, "I don't know". Instead, confidently explain why you don't know this specific point and reassure them you will look into it and get back to them about it.

Not knowing something doesn't make you a bad leader; but what can make you a great one is studying up on the unfamiliar subjects and informing others about your findings. When you refuse to admit that you are wrong, you are exhibiting a weakness, which is not a trait of a leader. You must put aside your pride, you are still a person after all, and none of us know everything at all times.

The goal is not to know everything, it is to feel comfortable and to be seen as an expert in your field. Remember when you were taught that knowledge is power? Take every opportunity to keep refining your knowledge. We all know it is impossible to know everything, but you can make your best effort to know your field. Something that breaks your team's trust is when you make up an answer and they find out later that it was not true. Never lie to your team in order to persuade them of your intelligence, it will only backfire and end up ruining your credibility.

Commitment
"You may have to fight a battle more than once to win it." - Margaret Thatcher

Showing that you are committed to your personal growth will give you a bonus point in leadership. As soon as you and your team start to improve, so will everything else in and around your organization. In some companies, leaders pay their employees to read books and take courses that improve their lives, both personally and professionally. Keep this tip in mind, try to start programs that benefit the personal and professional lives and your team and colleagues. It will amaze you how effective it can be at increasing productivity.

A great leader is always looking for ways to improve their leadership skills and to develop their own self-discipline to succeed in their role as leader. A good leader will want to foster the same key attributes in those they are leading. A key trait that every leader must have is self-discipline. It is a requirement if you want to execute a goal in your workspace. Before you can practice discipline with your team, you must have good discipline yourself. Without discipline, it is no use having a vision or good ideas; the execution lies in the discipline. In addition to discipline, leaders must also exhibit a variety of qualities including:

- Constantly ask yourself how you can prove yourself to be an asset

- Leaders must not be silent, but know when to be quiet

- A good leader has nothing to prove, but everything to improve

- Must not be foolhardy but show appropriate courage

- Leaders must be bold and decisive, but also show endurance

- Leaders must be confident enough without overstepping the line

- Must be competitive, but celebrating other people's failures divides followers from leaders

- You do not qualify to lead if you rebel against higher authority

There are certain traits and preferences that make you the person you are. These are individual aspects of your personality that can either add to or subtract from the substance you offer a company. The more in touch with yourself that you are, the easier you will find this to be, it will become much easier to identify key traits about yourself that make you valuable.

Make it a priority to develop a management style that pulls in desirable professional traits and complements them with valuable feminine traits such as a nurturing mentality and intuition. When developing your management style, keep these five simple personal rules in mind:

- Work hard and be willing to do the work that nobody else wants to do

- Work with the people in charge, not against them

- Know what you want out of life and go after it

- Be authentic as you promote yourself and connect with your peers

- Never develop a fear of changing your mind

Sometimes we get started on an objective and the path forks. In fact, many current female CEOs had different career paths before turning toward the C-suite. So never be afraid to change the course of direction if you no longer feel fulfilled in a workplace or career type.

Remember that you will get nowhere with a "can't" mentality, but you can create miracles with a "can" mindset.

Keep your eyes on your long-term goals and realize that they will take time to reach. One of the first changes you should make when aspiring to improve is to realize that your mental outlook plays a dramatic role in your success. You must cultivate the mindset of a leader by focusing on building specific skills and training your brain to focus on what you are capable of rather than only seeing the challenges in front of you. Create intentional habits that will foster the strengthening of your character and leadership capabilities.

Having a vision
"A vision is not just a picture of what could be; it is an appeal to our better selves, a call to become something more." - Rosabeth Moss Kanter

Having the right vision is very important as a leader. It may be easy to get caught up in all the challenges that lay ahead when you run a company, but always keep the bigger picture in mind, this is your vision. Do not just look at your immediate goals, look at both present and future. If you have a narrow-minded view, this can with time compromise your promotability. Set up a clear vision to ensure long-term success and follow it.

How do we balance all of this? This is likely one of your strengths as a woman. We are experts when it comes to making a balanced decision. Women have various roles in their lives, they are sisters, wives, mothers etc. This alone has trained women's brains to be wise when it comes to making decisions. Realize and accept the various sacrifices you will have to make in order to reach your goals and grow a thick skin when you hear the criticisms about those decisions. Not everyone will see eye to eye with your aspirations and that means that you may hear people talking negatively about your family choices, how you rear your children, or whether you choose to get married. You cannot allow those statements to deter you or break down your confidence. In order to develop that strength, you must continually work to develop yourself into the person you most desire to be, no matter what others may do, think, or say.

When reflecting about the possibility of becoming a CEO, look inward and remember to consider your motivations for desiring this role and its many opportunities and responsibilities. When you are doing this take some time to think about if you would prefer working in the private or public sector and what types of industries interest you most. Everyone's heard the age-old saying about work not being "work" if you are doing what you love, and even in a position of leadership and duty, a woman can still strive to work in the fields that appeal to her the most. Don't be afraid of trying out new fields, for example, more and more women are becoming interested in technical positions.

Let other employees and leaders know about your aspirations. If nobody knows you have a desire to move into a role with more responsibility, you are much less likely to move forward into that role. Also, keep in mind that you don't have to wait for the opportunity to come across your path. We need to rely on our network and speak up for our dreams to come true. This is where recalling that fortune often favors the bold is crucial, so don't be afraid to speak up when you have interesting or helpful ideas. It shows that you are brave enough to take charge and are willing to take risks within reason.

Ask yourself, how can you make the company better? In what ways can you add some value to projects and make them better? From that starting point, begin to develop methods that a CEO would showcase. Behave and think like a CEO and teach yourself all the needed facets that go along with being a CEO. You will want to gain as much management experience as possible, so study it extensively and adopt the tips outlined in this book to make yourself a valuable manager.

Being prepared for the job
"It takes as much energy to wish as it does to plan." - Eleanor Roosevelt

Going back to being over-prepared; it's a great idea to have your pitch ready, along with a cover letter and resume that is board-ready. While it isn't necessary to have a college degree from Ivy League School as we discussed, it helps if you focus your studies on a field that is related to your industry, or to business or management. Here are several practical tips to make sure you are prepared for the job:

- Find someone to mentor and sponsor you

- Be persistent because it is that determination that will capture the attention of the people needed to realize your dreams

- Make sure you possess flexibility and resilience, you may have to bend in ways that are unexpected. Master this, it's one of the crucial aspects a leader needs to possess

- Always maintain a good attitude and graciousness because your mindset can alienate you from good opportunities or open you up to them

Taking a bit of initiative will go a long way. Most employees are given tasks that they have proven to be good at. So, don't wait for more responsibilities to be handed to you, go above and beyond your current position. Having the mindset that you know what your role and responsibilities are, will not alone assert your leadership; show that you can think outside the box on your own.

- Try to learn as much as you can, remember, the more you do the more you learn

- The more you experience the more you absorb, so make yourself available to those opportunities that you may not always be drawn to

- Be constantly be evolving and learning. Once you do this you can demonstrate the ability to move those skills you have honed and perfected in your previous specialist roles into a position of leadership that extends across disciplines. This will make you worth your weight in gold to a company looking for maturity and tact

- Never hesitate to ask questions and always consider yourself as a leader

Showing the discipline needed to self-educate and self-develop your skills and talents isn't something that anyone else will encourage you to do. It is something you must train yourself to do. Remember that when you become a candidate for the C-suite, you will always need to be playing your A-game. How do you do that? By first realizing that it will be a long journey, a haul of many hurdles and obstacles before you finally reach CEO status. Then apply the tactics in this book to the develop your own personal strategy for success. In summary, women who strive to become members of the C-suite, all seem to have five core traits in common regardless of their industry. Here are five crucial points to help you reach those goals:

- Establish your own management style

- Have strong communication skills

- Possess a strong sense of inner confidence

- Be well educated in the appropriate areas

- Have a clear vision for success and a sense of self-discipline

Chapter 6: Fulfillment of dreams is the fulfillment of self

"Every great dream begins with a dreamer. Always remember, you have within you the strength, the patience, and the passion to reach for the stars to change the world." - Harriet Tubman

The fact of the matter is that everyone has some inner dream they hope to achieve. The problem with dreams is that most people cannot visualize a way, an actual path, to achieve them, so they assume they are impossible. Visualizing your path to the CEO position is not important, what is important is knowing that you can get there.

There are many training programs and opportunities to learn something, but this only provides a foundation. You have to work to gain practical experience; this is a step that many women fail to take because it involves risk and potential failure. A prime example of this can be seen by looking at how many young marriages end because young women become tired of staying home and caring for the children and the house.

Even many women who do go to college and earn degrees often put those degrees on the back burner once they have families and children to concern themselves with. There is nothing wrong with this and it can be a noble pursuit, unfortunately, the problem with this is that it ultimately leaves many women feeling trapped in a life that they did not create for themselves. They love their families and children, so they sacrifice their inner voice and goals without giving it a second thought. Then their children grow, and their spouses change in various ways and they are left to look at the remnants of their life and wonder what to do next.

This all comes down to a simple fact; fulfilling your dreams is the key to having a sense of fulfillment in the long run. Rising to the calling of what you feel you should do in life will give you a revival and an opportunity to thrive instead of merely surviving.

Solidify your dream
"When you have a dream, you've got to grab it and never let go." – Carol Burnett

Don´t listen to other´s people dreams for you, decide what you truly want and focus on that. If oppression is ever to be abolished, it is crucial to look at your life and think about what you really want to achieve. A report published by the Pew Research Center in 2018 indicated that the number of CEO women in Fortune 500 companies reached its highest value of 6.7% in the year 2017. This percentage relates to 32 women as the head of renowned firms. In 2018, however, this percentage dropped to only 4.8% following the resignation of many women in top positions. (Center 2018). If you have the inclination to work toward a CEO position, now is the time to make your move. The world needs you to take the reins now more than ever before, we are at a pivotal point in history and your dream of getting to the C-suite is attainable. Roadblocks and challenges will arise multiple times, but continue visualizing yourself as the leader you know yourself to be.

Realize that it takes hard work, dedication and a lot of patience to break through barriers that have existed for centuries. You must be a trailblazing pioneer who is not afraid to trudge through the trenches to reach the finish line. Face your fears, pursue your dreams, and find the most successful version of yourself.

Putting yourself first
"Never make someone a priority when all you are to them is an option." - Maya Angelou

Putting yourself last happens when you cease to focus on your dreams. The problem is that many women feel like putting their dreams first is selfish. This is not true. If you are working hard to accomplish the tasks for your household and family, you are doing the right thing, but that does not mean you should not be able to pursue your full potential and seek bigger opportunities in life. Ask yourself if what you are doing is all there is to life or if you have sold yourself short, then reassess what you are doing and make the changes needed to make your dream tangible.

Often it's just a little thing you need to address, and you can begin to feel proud of who you are. Think about how the powerhouse women have risen to the challenge of revamping their lives and still maintaining their ideal work-life balances. Consider the methods they use. Look at how these women have a greater sense of self because of the ways they've developed their lives to live the best of both worlds; try to create your own method to do the same. You do not have to settle for less just because it is safe or because you feel secure with things as they are.

Remember, stepping out of your comfort zone is what will allow doors to open. It isn't just about finding your voice, speaking up, and being heard; it is also about being willing to be true to yourself and realizing when you feel dissatisfied, then taking the step to move forward from there. Even if you just read this book out of curiosity and never intended on obtaining a CEO role, you may now feel like you are able to do so. Take a moment to listen to your inner voice because that intuition will lead you to live your happiest life.

Pay attention and learn to listen to your intuition and work toward building a life in a way that you feel proud of. Let your personal values be a guide. Try to be clear on what you want to do by outlining what it is you feel most passionate about. Take those guidelines forward throughout life and stick to them and never compromise your morality for an opportunity. Keep in mind that no matter what happens in life, everything eventually passes. Nothing lasts forever and you may make some mistakes, but what molds your character is how you rise from those mistakes.

There are certain traits that all leaders possess that you must adopt for yourself. Leadership is not a gender role, but one where a person can take full accountability for themselves and the people beneath them. Part of that comes from having a deep sense of knowing themselves. You must first build a platform of belief and then support those beliefs by being proactive about the things you know you can improve.

Some of the ways that women have had an edge over men are because of their ability to recognize their own emotions and the emotions of their team members. These are the women who stand out because they are not only nurturing, but they are also willing to take the needed risks at the appropriate time to assert their thoughts. Women with vision and flexibility who learn quickly know how to adapt to their male counterparts and utilize not only their similarities but their differences to gain an advantage.

It's going to be a long road, but stop thinking about the things you can´t do and start assessing what you can. If you limit yourself by never trying to do something, you will never get the chance to do it.

REFERENCES

AGRAWAL, KIMBERLY FITCH AND SANGEETA. 2014. *Why Women Are Better Managers Than Men.* Research finding , Business Journal, US.

Alexis Krivkovich, Marie-Claude Nadeau, Kelsey Robinson, Nicole Robinson, Irina Starikova, and Lareina Yee. 2018. *Women in the Workplace 2018.* McKinsey & Company.

Blumberg, Yoni. 2018. *Companies with more female executives make more money—here's why.* CNBC.

Catalyst. 2018. *Women in Management.* research finding , Catalyst .

Center, Pew Research. 2018. *The Data on Women Leaders.* Washington: Pew Research Center.

College, Nichols. 2019. *Tracking Issues in Women's Leadership.* Institute for Women's Leadership.

Ellingrud, Kweilin. 2019. *How Women Leaders Change Company Dynamics.* Forbes.

Judith Warner, Nora Ellmann, Diana Boesch. 2018. *The Women's Leadership Gap.* Center for American Progress.

Scarborough, William. 2018. *What the Data Says About Women in Management Between 1980 and 2010.* Gender Resarch , Havard Business Revies.

Schneider, Michael. 2018. *40 Years of Research Proves Women Are Better Managers Than Men Because They Tend to Have This Crucial Skill.* Research findinds, Manuseto Ventures .

University, Maryville. 2019. *Leadership Tools and Resources for Women Managers, Executives, and Entrepreneurs.* Maryville University.

Zipkin, Nina. 2018. *Women Are Still Not Being Offered Management Positions at Equal Rates, But There's Hope, Sheryl Sandberg Says.* Women Entrepreneur .

www.ingramcontent.com/pod-product-compliance
Lightning Source LLC
Chambersburg PA
CBHW021441210526
45463CB00002B/606